SUPER SPORTS STAR
PENNY HARDAWAY

Ken Rappoport

Enslow Publishers, Inc.

40 Industrial Road   PO Box 38
Box 398   Aldershot
Berkeley Heights, NJ 07922   Hants GU12 6BP
USA   UK

http://www.enslow.com

Library of Congress Cataloging-in-Publication Data

Rappoport, Ken.
Super sports star Penny Hardaway / Ken Rappoport.
   p. cm. — (Super sports star)
Includes bibliographical references (p.) and index.
ISBN 0-7660-1516-5
1. Hardaway, Anfernee—Juvenile literature. 2. Basketball players—United States—Biography—Juvenile literature. [1. Hardaway, Anfernee. 2. Basketball players—United States—Biography. 3. Afro-Americans—Biography.] I. Title. II. Series.
GV884.H24 R38 2001

796.323'092–dc21

   00-011441

Printed in the United States of America

10 9 8 7 6 5 4 3 2 1

To Our Readers:
All Internet addresses in this book were active and appropriate when we went to press. Any comments or suggestions can be sent by e-mail to Comments@enslow.com or to the address on the back cover.

Photo Credits: Allen Einstein/NBA Photos, p. 24; Andrew D. Bernstein/NBA Photos, pp. 4, 36, 45; Barry Gossage/NBA Photos, pp. 6, 7, 10, 17, 19, 26, 31, 33; Chris Covatta/NBA Photos, p 1; Fernando Medina/NBA Photos, pp. 12, 22, 42; Gregg Forwerck/NBA Photos, p. 34; Jerry Wachter/NBA Photos, pp. 28, 38; Lou Capozzola/NBA Photos, p. 39; Nathaniel S. Butler/NBA Photos, pp. 8, 15; Sam Forencich/NBA Photos, p. 29.

Cover Photo: Chris Covatta/NBA Photos

CONTENTS

Introduction

Putting Anfernee "Penny" Hardaway's basketball talents into words is almost as difficult as trying to stop his moves to the basket. Is he a point guard? Is he a shooting guard? Or is he a forward? Actually, he is all three.

Penny Hardaway, star guard for the Phoenix Suns, has been compared to Magic Johnson. Like the former Los Angeles Lakers great, he is a big guard who can do many things.

The six-foot seven-inch Hardaway can set up the offense from the point guard position. He can shoot from outside and inside. He can dunk and rebound like a forward. He is also good on defense.

Penny Hardaway has also been compared to Michael Jordan for his creative style on the court. The modest Hardaway prefers to make his own mark in NBA history. And, he is on his way. Like Magic Johnson and Michael Jordan, Penny Hardaway has never stopped working to be the best.

Penny Hardaway is very valuable to the Phoenix Suns. He is a big guard who can do many things on the court.

Up, Up, and Away!

CHAPTER 1

Could Anfernee "Penny" Hardaway save the Orlando Magic? He was an all-star guard in the National Basketball Association (NBA). But it seemed that not even Superman could help the Magic.

The Magic had lost the first two games of the 1997 playoffs to the Miami Heat. One more loss and the Magic would be out. The Magic had also lost important players to injuries. No one expected the team to

Penny Hardaway is an unselfish player. Part of his job is to set up plays so that teammates can score.

win the series against Miami. Some called the Magic "quitters."

That was exactly the way they looked in Game 3. The Magic were losing, 39–19, in the second period. Then starting center Rony Seikaly went out of the game with a leg injury.

"I guess you could say I got a little angry," Hardaway said. He made a decision. "Miami was going to know it had been in a fight."

What happened next?

Penny Hardaway had always been known as an unselfish player. He did not care how many points he scored. His job as a point guard was to set up plays. He was happy when his pass to a teammate resulted in a basket.

But now he had to change. He needed to help his team win games. He needed to score points himself. And that is what he did.

He scored 15 straight points. At one time in the first half, he scored 28 of Orlando's 34 points. He was all over the court. In addition to

Hardaway prepares to put the ball through the hoop. He has proven that he can be a team leader on the court.

scoring, he rebounded and played tough defense. He did it all.

"It's one of the best performances I've ever seen Penny have," Magic coach Richie Adubato said.

Hardaway finished with 42 points and 8 rebounds. He helped the Magic beat the Heat, 88–75.

He was not finished, though. The next game was another big night for him. He had 41 points, 7 rebounds, and 4 assists. The Magic won again, 99–91. They had tied the series at two wins for each team.

Hardaway was on a roll. In Game 5, he scored 33 points. But the Heat were too much for the Magic. Orlando lost the deciding game, 91–83.

Still, the Magic had shown courage. And Penny Hardaway had shown that he could change into a team leader.

Growing Up With Grandma

As a child, Penny Hardaway was raised by a very strict grandmother. He lived in a small house in a poor neighborhood in Memphis, Tennessee.

"She used to make me get out of bed at 6 A.M., even when I didn't have school," Penny remembered of his grandmother, Louise Hardaway. He always had to clean his room and do his chores. He had to eat breakfast before he could do anything else.

His grandmother made the rules: schoolwork first, then play. Penny brought home A's and B's. He also brought home bumps and scrapes from fights with the other kids. Kids would pick on him because they thought he was different. "They thought I was a nerd," said Hardaway.

Penny's grandmother gave her grandson the

★★★ **UP CLOSE**
★

When he was born on July 18, 1971, he was named Anfernee. In a strong southern accent, Louise Hardaway would call her grandson "pretty." But it sounded like "penny" to his friends. Everyone started calling him Penny.

following advice: "Stay focused and keep your dreams. One day they will come true."

Penny dreamed of being a football player. One day he and his grandmother were watching a football game on television. "As thin as you are, they'd break every bone in your body," his grandmother said. "Basketball is dangerous, but not like football."

Basketball came naturally to Penny. By the time he was ten years old, he was playing with the older guys in the neighborhood. He learned from them. These "playground coaches" gave Penny a new goal. Now he dreamed of becoming the next Julius Erving, Magic Johnson, or Larry Bird. They were the great stars of the NBA.

What happened next seemed like a dream. Penny had scored 70 points in a Boys Club basketball game. The high school coach invited Penny to join the high school team. He was only in ninth grade, and already playing on the varsity (high school) team.

When he was a young boy, Penny Hardaway dreamed of becoming the next Julius Erving, Magic Johnson, or Larry Bird. They were all great stars of the NBA.

Penny had never seen a high school basketball game before putting on that varsity uniform. But he quickly became the star of the team. He was a hero in basketball-crazy Memphis.

Should a hero have to hand in school assignments? Penny did not think so. He let his schoolwork slide. He failed two classes in his final year of high school. He was not allowed to play basketball for part of the season.

Fans called him a "dumb jock." Hardaway wanted to play college ball at Memphis State. But he would not be able to do it because his grades were too low.

What was Hardaway going to do?

Books and Basketball

Penny Hardaway could hit the backboards. But could he hit the books? That was the challenge facing him now.

He was going to college. He had been accepted at Memphis State University in Tennessee. He had been accepted under a special program called "Proposition 48," but there was a catch. Hardaway could not play basketball until he improved his grades. So for the first year of college, he was just a student. His low grades in high school embarrassed him. "They're calling you dumb," his grandmother said. "Don't let those folks make a fool out of you."

He never expected what happened next. One day, he was visiting his old neighborhood with a friend. Four men jumped out of a car. They had guns, and they ordered Penny and his friend to lie down. The robbers took their sneakers, jewelry, and wallets. Then the robbers drove away, firing shots out of the car

When Penny Hardaway was still in college, Magic Johnson once compared Hardaway's style of play to his own unique court style.

windows. One of the bullets hit Penny in the leg. It broke three bones.

In the hospital, Penny had time to think. He knew he was lucky to be alive. He studied harder than ever. He made the dean's list, a special honor for students with very good grades. And, best of all, he was allowed to play on the basketball team.

When Memphis State coach Larry Finch first saw Hardaway at practices, he was amazed. Hardaway could shoot, pass, rebound, and play defense. He did so many things well, it was hard to know what position he should play. He solved the problem by playing everywhere. He set up plays as the "point" guard. He scored three-point shots from long range. He scored from short range on dunk shots. He played like a forward and swept up rebounds. As a sophomore, in his second year, he was called the best all-around college player in America.

Hardaway received special praise after playing in an exhibition game against the

United States Olympic "Dream Team." Magic Johnson said, "At times I thought I was looking in a mirror. He reminds me of myself so much."

Hardaway's Memphis State Tigers played in a league called the Great Midwest Conference. He was twice named the league's Player of the Year. He was an Associated Press All-American. He led the Tigers to the postseason tournament of the National Collegiate Athletic Association (NCAA). He did it all for Memphis State. Now he was ready to move up to the pros.

Hardaway announced he would be leaving school one year early to join the NBA. Coach Finch had seen him turn the Tigers around. Could Hardaway turn around a pro team?

CHAPTER 4

A Magical Showing

It was show time. Penny Hardaway was on center stage in a gym in Orlando, Florida. The audience included team officials from the Orlando Magic.

It was just twenty-four hours before the 1993 NBA draft. The draft is the way that teams pick new players each year. The Magic had the first pick in the draft. They were all set to pick Chris Webber. He was regarded as the top player in college. He was from Michigan.

But was he the player for the Magic? Hardaway did not think so.

"I was convinced they were one guard away from making the playoffs," the confident Hardaway said. "I was that guard."

But Hardaway had to convince the Magic. And, he had to do it in a pickup game against some of the Magic's star players.

The Magic had seen Hardaway at an earlier tryout. They were impressed, but Webber was still their first choice.

Penny Hardaway dreamed about playing on

Before becoming a member of the Magic, Penny Hardaway dreamed about playing on the same team with Shaquille O'Neal.

the same team with Shaquille O'Neal. He asked for a second tryout. Finally the Magic agreed to watch him play again.

Penny Hardaway was a great college player. But now he had to be even better. He had to make the pros change their minds. It would not be easy. The twenty-year-old Hardaway only had ninety minutes to prove himself.

He showed them his best moves. He passed the ball. He took all kinds of shots from all over the court. He rebounded the ball. He dazzled the more experienced players. And he dazzled general manager Pat Williams. Williams said he "saw a dozen things" that would have excited the Magic fans.

Hardaway had put on a great show, but he still felt the Magic would pick Webber. And he was right. When the draft opened, the Magic selected the Michigan star. Penny was disappointed. He was picked by the Golden State Warriors.

He and Chris Webber were surprised by

Hardaway goes up for the shot over the outstretched arm of his defender.

what happened next. The Magic suddenly announced they had traded Webber to Golden State for Hardaway. Chris Webber was going to play for Golden State and Hardaway was going to play for Orlando. The Warriors also sent three future draft choices to Orlando. Hardaway's dream had come true. He was now a member of the Orlando Magic.

The Magic's fans had cheered when their team selected Webber. They booed when the Magic announced the trade.

Hardaway had won over the Magic. Now he had to win over the fans. And he had to help his new team win more games.

Penny's Big Test

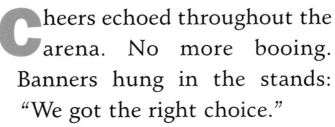

Cheers echoed throughout the arena. No more booing. Banners hung in the stands: "We got the right choice."

"It made me want to go out and play as hard as I could," Hardaway said. The support inspired him.

It was only the fifth home game of the 1993–94 season for the Orlando Magic. For Hardaway, it was his biggest test. The opponent was the Golden State Warriors. In the minds of many Magic fans, it was really Penny Hardaway against Chris Webber.

Hardaway did not give the fans a chance to

In his first game against Chris Webber, Penny Hardaway put on a great performance.

boo him. He had a great all-around game. He had 23 points, 8 rebounds, 5 assists, and 2 blocked shots. Webber was held to 13 points by Shaquille O'Neal. The Magic won, 120–107.

"If I [had scored] only four points and he'd hit 25, I would have never heard the end of it," Hardaway said.

With Hardaway and O'Neal together, the Magic had a great pair of players. O'Neal was already one of the NBA's top centers. Hardaway was still a first-year player, but he was showing signs he could be one of the top guards. He was gaining confidence with each passing day. After two months, he had taken over the position of starting guard from Scott Skiles.

Then Hardaway took

★★★ UP CLOSE

Shaquille O'Neal had been the first pick for the Magic in the 1992 NBA draft. He led the Magic to their best record since they came into the NBA in 1989. But he could not lead them to the playoffs. In their short history, the team had never played in the postseason. Penny Hardaway helped change that.

In just his first year in the NBA, Penny Hardaway's hard work on the court paid off.

over the NBA's rookie All-Star Game. He scored 22 points. He was named the game's Most Valuable Player. The Magic thought he could be the answer. By the All-Star break, the Magic were twelve games over .500. They were playoff-bound.

The Indiana Pacers knocked them out in the first round. But the season had been a breakthrough for both the Magic and Penny Hardaway. The Magic had made the playoffs for the first time. And Penny Hardaway received the Magic Fans' Choice Award as the team's most popular player. He had finally won over the fans.

A Shining Star

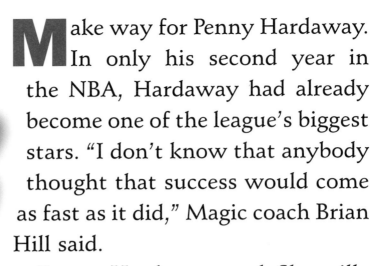

Make way for Penny Hardaway. In only his second year in the NBA, Hardaway had already become one of the league's biggest stars. "I don't know that anybody thought that success would come as fast as it did," Magic coach Brian Hill said.

Penny Hardaway and Shaquille O'Neal helped the Magic become the best team in the Eastern Conference. Hardaway loved playing with O'Neal. They also played in the midseason All-Star Game. But starting in the All-Star Game was one thing. Could Hardaway help the Magic all by himself? He was going to get the chance.

Hardaway appears to fly through the air as he goes up for the shot.

It was a February night in 1995 in Orlando. The Magic were facing the great Chicago Bulls. Shaquille O'Neal was not in the game. He had been suspended for one game. Horace Grant and Brian Shaw were not playing, either. They were injured.

The score was tied at 103. Hardaway picked up a loose ball at the Chicago foul line. He raced the length of the court. There were only a few seconds left. He started his leap toward the basket.

He brought the ball up over his head and slammed it through the hoop with one second left. The game buzzer sounded. The Magic had beaten the Bulls, 105–103. Penny Hardaway had scored a career-high 39 points.

It was one of fifty-seven victories for the Magic during the 1994–95 season. It was a team record. Only the San Antonio Spurs in the Western Conference had a better record that season. The Magic were on their way to the playoffs. They did not want to repeat the mistakes of the 1994 playoffs.

In the first round of the NBA playoffs, teams play a five-game series. The first to win

Penny Hardaway shoots over the arms of his defender. His consistent play helped the Orlando Magic advance to the playoffs in 1995.

three games goes on to the second round. The Magic had failed to win even one game against Indiana in 1994. "That left a bitter taste in our mouths for a long time," Penny said.

In 1995, the Magic won their first-round series. They beat Boston. Then they beat Chicago and the great Michael Jordan. Finally they beat Indiana to advance to the NBA Finals.

Orlando's magical ride finally stopped when the Magic were beaten by the Houston Rockets in the Finals. Penny Hardaway looked ahead to a new season. Things might be different then. They were, but in a way Hardaway could not have imagined.

On His Own

I want to be the best player in basketball," Penny Hardaway said as he prepared for the 1995–96 NBA season.

He worked hard over the summer. He came back to training camp stronger than ever. The Orlando Magic needed Hardaway in top shape. There was no Shaquille O'Neal, at least for a while. The Magic's star center had a broken thumb.

Hardaway faced a big test early in the season. The Magic took on the Chicago Bulls and Michael Jordan.

Hardaway started hitting his shots. Jordan was guarding Hardaway, but he could not stop him from scoring. It was a great performance. Penny Hardaway scored 36 points on his way to a dazzling performance against the world-famous superstar, Michael Jordan. Hardaway also had 5 rebounds and 4 steals. The final score was, Orlando 94, Chicago

The start of the 1995–96 season found Hardaway working without the help of Shaquille O'Neal. O'Neal broke his thumb and would not be able to play for a while.

88, and Hardaway had come through for his team.

"I'm still learning," Hardaway said after the game. But he was learning fast. Hardaway was leading the team. The Magic had a 17–5 record while O'Neal was away. It was a look into the future. The following year, O'Neal left the Magic to join the Los Angeles Lakers. The Orlando Magic was now Penny Hardaway's team.

"I know I have a load on my hands because teams are going to target me," Hardaway said. "Before, it was always, 'Get the ball to Shaq.' It's on my shoulders now. I've got to carry us."

After only four years in the NBA, Penny Hardaway was already a star. He was a member of the U.S. Olympic "Dream Team." He was a first-team All-NBA selection.

The future looked bright for the Magic and their all-star guard. His dazzling performance against Miami in the 1997 playoffs was a highlight. It proved how much he meant to his team. He was the one player the Magic could not afford to lose. But they did lose him. Hardaway injured his knee and needed surgery.

His playing time was limited over the next two seasons. The Magic struggled without their top player. There were rumors at the end of the 1998–99 season that the team would trade him.

Trade Penny Hardaway? Yes, to the Phoenix Suns.

"It was best for me to leave, just move on, start a new career," said Hardaway. He joined another superstar guard in Phoenix, Jason Kidd. They formed a strong backcourt.

"Now," Phoenix coach Danny Ainge said, "I really believe we're an elite team in the NBA."

Hardaway and the Suns went all the way to

★★★ **UP CLOSE**
★

Penny Hardaway had helped to make the Orlando Magic a strong team. And, when the time came, he was ready to do the same for the Phoenix Suns. He was off to a good start in his first game with Phoenix. In a game against Philadelphia on November 4, 1999, Hardaway had 18 points and 3 assists in an 84–80 win for Phoenix.

Penny Hardaway would have a bright future ahead of him with the Suns.

the playoffs in 2000. Hardaway hurt his knee in their first game against the San Antonio Spurs, but he played through the pain so that he could help his team. He showed courage. The Suns beat the Spurs, and made it to the Conference Semifinals against the Los Angeles Lakers. Despite some sharp shooting by Hardaway, the Suns did not win that series. But, Hardaway had shown why he was one of the NBA's great players.

CAREER STATISTICS

				🏀 NBA					
Year	**Team**	**GP**	**FG%**	**Reb.**	**Ast.**	**Stl.**	**Blk.**	**Pts.**	**PPG**
1993–94	Orlando	82	.466	439	544	190	51	1,313	16.0
1994–95	Orlando	77	.512	336	551	130	26	1,613	20.9
1995–96	Orlando	82	.513	354	582	166	41	1,780	21.7
1996–97	Orlando	59	.447	263	332	93	35	1,210	20.5
1997–98	Orlando	19	.377	76	68	28	15	311	16.4
1998–99	Orlando	50	.420	284	266	111	23	791	15.8
1999–2000	Phoenix	60	.474	347	315	94	38	1,015	16.9
Totals		**429**	**.473**	**2,099**	**2,658**	**812**	**229**	**8,033**	**18.7**

GP—Games Played
FG%—Field Goal Percentage
Reb.—Rebounds

Ast.—Assists
Stl.—Steals
Blk.—Blocked Shots

Pts.—Points
PPG—Points Per Game

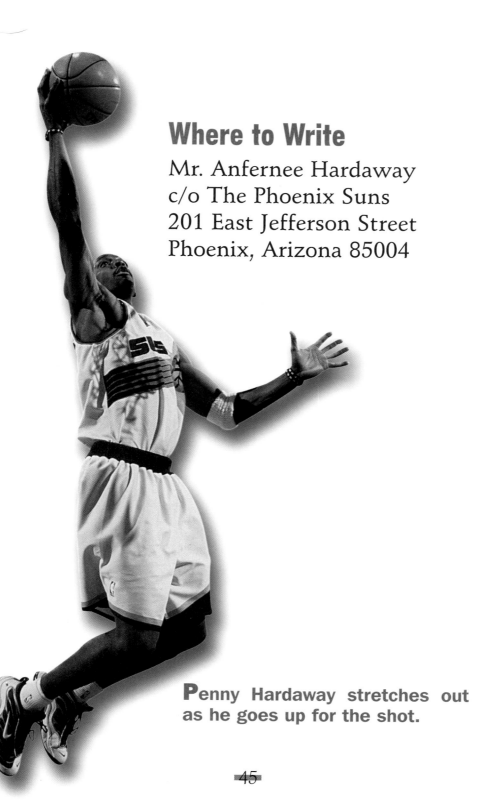

Where to Write

Mr. Anfernee Hardaway
c/o The Phoenix Suns
201 East Jefferson Street
Phoenix, Arizona 85004

Penny Hardaway stretches out as he goes up for the shot.

WORDS TO KNOW

center—The team's biggest player who does most of the rebounding and shot blocking.

"Dream Team"—The nickname for NBA players who made up the U.S. Olympic basketball teams.

forward—This player is bigger than the guard and plays in the "frontcourt." He is closer to the basket. Teams need forwards to rebound and score points.

guard—Usually the shortest player and best ball-handler on the team. The "point" guard controls the ball and sets up the plays. The second guard in the "backcourt" is counted on for scoring.

NBA—National Basketball Association.

NBA draft—The way that NBA teams pick new players each year.

NCAA—National Collegiate Athletic Association.

Proposition 48—A rule that allows student athletes with low grades to play sports in college. First they have to go to class for a year and improve their grades.

three-pointer—A basket that is scored from beyond the three-point line on the court, and counts for three points. The three-point line is about twenty feet from the hoop.

READING ABOUT

Books and Magazines

Clark, Brooks. "Magic Man! Penny Hardaway Dazzles the NBA." *Sports Illustrated For Kids*. December 1, 1995.

Daniels, Jeremy. *Anfernee Hardaway*. Broomall, Pa.: Chelsea House Publishers, Inc., 1996.

Gutman, Bill. *Anfernee Hardaway: Super Guard*. Brookfield, Conn.: The Millbrook Press Inc., 1997.

Joseph, Paul. *Anfernee Hardaway*. Minneapolis, Minn.: ABDO Publishing Company, 1998.

Rambeck, Richard. *Anfernee (Penny) Hardaway*. Chanhassen, Minn.: The Child's World, Inc., 1996.

Townsend, Brad. *Anfernee Hardaway: Basketball's Lucky Penny*. Minneapolis, Minn.: Lerner Publishing Group, 1997.

Internet Addresses

The Official Web Site of the NBA
<http://www.nba.com/playerfile/anfernee_hardaway.html>

The Official Web Site of the Phoenix Suns
<http://www.nba.com/Suns/>

INDEX